SHADES

A one act play

By

Kenneth Clelland

Best Wishes
Kenneth Clelland

FIRE CIRCLE PUBLISHING

© 2016 by Kenneth Clelland

The right Tim Jenkins as Kenneth Clelland to be identified as the Author of the Work has been asserted by him in accordance with the Copyright, Design and Patents Act 1988.

All rights whatsoever in this play are strictly reserved and application for permission to perform or reproduce in any form, print, stage, film etc., all or part of any of this play, must be made in advance, before rehearsals begin to:

Fire Circle Publishing, 9a Craddock's Parade, Ashtead, Surrey KT21 1QL

All characters in this publication and any resemblance to real persons living or dead is purely coincidental

ISBN: 978-0-9930313-2-8

Cover Design and text lay out by Tim Jenkins using Serif PagePlus and DrawPlus

Printed and bound in Great Britain by Clays Ltd, St Ives plc

Dedication

To my friends in Mole Valley
Scriptwriters' Group and the WEA
for their help and and support during
the development of this play.

SHADES

© Timothy H Jenkins as Kenneth Clelland.

Characters

In order of appearance

Mr. Ignis *(Estate Agent)*
Woman *(Bernice)*
Man *(Laurie)*

SHADES

The set is the interior of a property for sale. Time: any time in the last 50 years. The room has the look of being part of an old family home. There are several doors. The foot and first few steps of a staircase are visible. The furnishings are old, of quality and probably passed down. There is an easy chair and matching settee. There are sundry pieces of furniture with ornaments, pictures, etc. A man of a swarthy complexion, dressed in a long, black raincoat and dark trousers, with almost black hair with a widow's peek, accompanied by a young woman in her thirties, dressed casually, enter through the main door leaving the door open behind them. The man is an estate agent and she is viewing the property. She looks the room over. The room is only dimly lit to begin with. It gets brighter as the scene develops. There is another man in the room but somehow he is invisible to them. He is about the same age as the woman, and dressed in shades of grey. The woman is a trifle fey but with a hard edge.

MR IGNIS. This is the main reception and sitting room.

WOMAN. Not bad! Not bad at all.

MR IGNIS. It's a fine property.

WOMAN. You know I fell in love with it the moment I saw it in your window.

MR IGNIS. It's not been lived in for some years.

WOMAN. Why not?

MR IGNIS. I can't say.

WOMAN. A secret?

MR IGNIS. No. I don't think so. It's probably something quite mundane. Probate, I expect.

WOMAN. How disappointing. A mystery would have been so much more fun.

MR IGNIS. I've only recently joined the company.

WOMAN. Could you see what you can dig up for me? I'd like to know the history of the place.

MR IGNIS. I'll enquire back at the office. I'm sure that you'll have little difficulty finding out.

WOMAN. The neighbours you mean?

MR IGNIS. Possibly.

WOMAN. Well what ever you can find out …

MR IGNIS. I'll certainly do my best.

WOMAN. Thanks, I'm sure you will. *(starting to look around).*

Now this is what I meant by a place with atmosphere.

MR IGNIS. I'm glad you think so.

WOMAN. It just reeks of it. No hidden problems, I hope?

MR IGNIS. There is nothing structurally wrong with it. All surveys have been quite satisfactory.

WOMAN. You have had others interested?

MR IGNIS. Oh yes. But for one reason or other they all changed their minds at the last minute.

WOMAN. A mystery after all. Perhaps the house didn't like them and it's been waiting for me.

MR IGNIS. Perhaps.

(He slips out of the door unnoticed by the woman)

WOMAN. I like the furniture too ... Odd though, I thought it was empty - not lived in for years, you said?

(She wanders around the room examining everything; in particular she picks up a framed photo, studies it for a moment then replaces it.)

But it looks so lived in. And this furniture is … is so right. Like it belongs. I hope it's being sold with the house. It would be awful if all these lovely things were thrown out. Like vandalism. It wouldn't be complete without them. The price is a bit more than I had in mind so I hope they are open to negotiation?

(She looks round and is surprised to discover she is on her own)

Mr Ignis? Strange. Mr Ignis?

(calling louder)

Mr Ignis, Mr Ignis ?

(She returns to the door and looks out, calling.)

Mr Ignis! Where's he gone?

(turning back into the room)

Oh well, I suppose ... got it to myself.

(She sits on a settee.)

Yes I feel comfortable here, like I belong here too. Feels lived in ... it's almost like I'd be sharing it.

(The door she came in through slams shut.)

Oh Mr Ignis!

(She jumps up startled and looks round, expecting to see him.)

Ah hah! A response.

(She smiles as she looks around the room.)

Trying to talk to me are you?

Even from the outside I felt I liked the place.

(Beginning to wander round the room again) I really believe I could be happy here. It's like I've known you ... for always. Every ornament, every picture. *(She picks up the framed photo again and replaces it)*

(The room is a bit lighter now.)

(Looking around with a new wonder) I'm sure all these things were here when I arrived ... yet somehow in a strange way it's like I'm just starting to see them. Sort of remember them. From when, from where ... I don't know. So long ago, so very long ago. *(lost in thought)* I seem to remember the whole house. But that's absurd - how could I? If I do, the dining room is through there.

(She crosses to the door down l. and opens it.)

Yes. Just as I thought. And I can see the conservatory beyond.

(with great satisfaction)

Yes. Just as I remember. But how could I? I've never been here before.

(She looks around, confused) This is silly. *(seeing a third door).* But I'm sure the kitchen is through there.

(She moves to the door and opens it.) Yes it is. *(pause)*

But how the hell did I know it?

(as if addressing the room itself and moving gradually down stage)

Tell me. How do I know you? *(looking about her)*

I know the whole house ... every room, downstairs and up. My beautiful bedroom. What am I saying? It must be a dream. *(shouting)* How can I know it all? HOW?

MAN   *(very quietly but clearly).* Because it's yours.

WOMAN *(She looks in the direction of the voice but the man remains invisible to her).* Mr Ignis? Was that you?

(She rushes to the door and opens it.)

WOMAN *(shouting and looking everywhere).* This isn't funny, Mr Ignis.

(She pauses, visibly shaken, tries to gather herself. She deliberately closes the door. The Man moves.)

WOMAN *(looking back into the room).* This is absurd. Who spoke to me?

MAN *(still clear, distant but deliberate)*. It was me.

(As she starts searching for him, he keeps moving so that she can't get a fix on him, but his voice level gradually increases.)

WOMAN *(gaining courage)*. And who the hell is 'me' when they're at home?

MAN.   I am at home.

WOMAN. What does that mean?

(There is a long silence. Angry, the woman, moves around the room looking for clues.)

WOMAN.   This is a silly game... Where are you hiding?

MAN.   Cold.

(The MAN, still moving, meets all her various attempts to find it with "COLD")

WOMAN. You must be somewhere.

(She tries doors at random.)

Come on out. Don't be silly you can't stay hidden. I'll find you eventually. *(Sing-song)* Come out, come out, wherever you are.

MAN *(on the move)*. Cold. Cold. Cold.

WOMAN *(then desperately)*. Look, don't mess about.

(There is a long silence)

Where the bloody hell are you?

MAN. Tut-tut. You haven't improved with age.

WOMAN. What? Are you saying that we've met before?

MAN. You'll have to see, won't you?

WOMAN *(screaming it).* I want answers for God's sake.

MAN. Blasphemy won't help.

WOMAN. I'm so sorry. Sensitive, aren't you? *(There is no response.)*

Where are you? *(There is again a long silence.)* Please answer me.

MAN. I can't.

WOMAN. What do you mean, you can't?

MAN. You have to ask the right question, then you might get an answer.

WOMAN. But I asked you a question. Where are you?

MAN. It wasn't the right one..

WOMAN. OK. *(She gives up looking and settles on the settee)* How about this then? Who are you?

MAN. Better. Someone who has been waiting for you.

WOMAN. That's not an answer.

MAN. It'll have to do for now.

WOMAN. Why don't you show yourself?

MAN. You aren't ready to see me yet.

WOMAN *(irritable)*. Must you talk in riddles?

MAN *(he is now talking at a normal level)*. I talk the only way you let me.

WOMAN. OK. *(carefully)* A straightforward question. Are you Mr Ignis?

MAN. Mr Fire. The man who brought you here?

WOMAN. Yes. Why did you call him Mr Fire?

MAN. Ignis is Latin for fire and no, of course I'm not him.

WOMAN. You'd better not be.

MAN. Do I sound like him?

WOMAN. No. But your voice does seem familiar.

MAN. So it should.

WOMAN. Why?

MAN. Only you can work that out.

WOMAN. OK, mister. It sounds as if you are in the room with me. So why can't I see you?

MAN. You told Mr Ignis that you liked mysteries.

WOMAN. It's got to be some trick. Hidden speakers or something.

MAN. Trick? There are no tricks.

WOMAN. So why can't I see you?

MAN. You will when you're ready.

WOMAN. Are you in here with me?

MAN. Would you like me to be?

WOMAN. I'd like to see who I'm talking to.

MAN. As I said, you will when you're ready.

WOMAN. I'm ready now. Show yourself.

MAN. If you were ready to see me, you would. You can't see me, so you're not ready.

WOMAN. OK, I'm not ready, *(leaping up)* but I am angry.

MAN. So it seems. You really must calm down.

WOMAN. Is that one of the conditions?

MAN. It's a good starting point.

WOMAN. To hell with you. I'm going.

(She makes for the main door, grabs the handle and pulls. It stays shut. She keeps trying but the door does not budge. She finally gives up)

WOMAN *(moving back into the room)*. It seems you don't want me to go.

MAN. It's you who doesn't want to go. You're in charge here.

WOMAN *(angry again)*. Of course I want to go.

(The door clicks open)

MAN *(quietly).* Madam. The door.

(See looks back at the open door but stays where she is.)

WOMAN *(calming down).* OK. I'll stay ... for now. *(She crosses to the door and closes it. Turns to face the room.)*

WOMAN. If you are here and I can't see you, *(She moves slowly down stage)* ... then you must be a ghost.

MAN. Do you believe in ghosts?

WOMAN. It's either that or you're making a fool of me.

MAN. I don't like the word ghost.

WOMAN. *(Turning upstage)* Oh really .

MAN. It suggests that I'm dead.

WOMAN. Well, are you?

MAN. We are carrying on a conversation. That in itself would seem to rule out the possibility of my being dead, wouldn't it?

WOMAN. I can't believe that I'm talking to a ghost.

MAN. Given the choice, I prefer 'shade'.

WOMAN. What's the difference?

MAN. A great deal. There is a lot more of you than there is of me. You are a rich shade of life. I am a pale shade of life, but a life just the same.

WOMAN. Good Lord, I think I can see you. Just the merest shadow, but yes.

MAN. There you are. Just as I said. I'm thickening up nicely. Keep this up and you will soon be able to see me properly.

WOMAN *(She moves slowly towards him).* It that really you?

MAN. It seems like it. This is the most substantial that I've been for a long time.

WOMAN *(Sitting on the arm of the settee).* How long have you been here?

MAN. Long enough.

WOMAN. That's not an answer.

MAN. It's the only one I've got.

WOMAN. How is it that I can remember this house and find your voice familiar if I've never in my life been here before?

MAN. Getting warmer.

WOMAN *(Pauses as an idea dawns).* Are you suggesting that I was here in some previous life.

MAN. That's one way of putting it.

WOMAN. But I don't believe in reincarnation, and I don't believe in ghosts. It's all rubbish. When you die, you die and that's it.

MAN. A little while ago you wouldn't have believed in me, but you must admit that you are happily talking to me now. Even starting to see me. You recognized the house, my presence here and the feel of the place as soon as you arrived. Let's face it, you wanted to believe. You even started the conversation.

WOMAN. My life is complicated enough without adding a previous existence.

MAN. Complicated? How?

WOMAN. It doesn't matter.

MAN. I'm sure it does.

WOMAN. Well if you're going to be secretive then so am I.

MAN. That's your decision.

WOMAN. If I was here in a previous life, tell me about it.

MAN. Against the rules. You have to remember.

WOMAN. How can I possibly do that? If there is such a thing as having a past life nobody can ever remember it.

MAN. Of course you can. You've already started remembering the house. The rest will come - in time.

WOMAN *(Getting up again to look around)*. I admit that the house seems oddly familiar but that's as far as my memory goes.

MAN. You remembered your bedroom ... 'My beautiful bedroom', you said.

WOMAN *(crossing to the foot of the stairs)*. Yes, but I've not been up stairs to confirm it.

MAN. Can you still remember it at this moment?

WOMAN. I can remember a room, somewhere.

MAN. It has a turret bay window built out at one corner.

WOMAN. Yes. It is a light room.

MAN. With windows at the back and side.

WOMAN. That could be any room.

MAN. All the windows are leaded but those on the north side have pink glass.

WOMAN. Yes. It gave the room warmth.

MAN. So you remember that too?

WOMAN. OK, so I recall that much, but I can't remember anything else. Nothing!

MAN. Then you are probably trying too hard.

WOMAN *(goes to chair and sits).* I'm not sure I want to remember.

MAN. Very possibly.

WOMAN *(uncomfortable).* Why don't I want to remember?

MAN. That's the crux, isn't it?

WOMAN. OK, I don't want to remember.

MAN. Like you don't want to know who I am?

WOMAN. How do you expect me to remember?

MAN. Let's talk about something else. That's usually a good way of stirring up memories.

WOMAN. Like what?

MAN. Where do you come from?

WOMAN. Today?

MAN. If you like.

WOMAN. Hampstead.

MAN. Is that your home?

WOMAN *(She pauses and sits).* Sort of.

MAN. You're unhappy there?

WOMAN *(dismissively).* Things change.

MAN. You used to be happy there?

WOMAN. I thought so... once.

MAN. What changed?

WOMAN. I don't know. It just stopped being ... ...as it was.

MAN. Explain.

WOMAN. I'm not sure I can.

(pause)

MAN. Were you on your own?

(She does not reply immediately but coils her legs up under her.)

WOMAN *(subdued).* I am now.

MAN. Ah! That's what changed.

WOMAN. That's what happened. Yes.

MAN. A lover?

WOMAN. We lived together.

MAN. And things didn't work out between you.

WOMAN *(Starting to uncoil)*. For a long time things were wonderful.

MAN. While love was fresh.

WOMAN *(Getting bigger)*. We had a world within a world.

MAN *(egging her on)*. Heaven on Earth?

WOMAN *(Not noticing his teasing and starting to enthuse)*. We were at one with life. With each other.

MAN *(sarcastically)*. You thought as one. You acted as one.

WOMAN *(defensively)* But we did. We did.

MAN. But you were being used. It was all a lie.

WOMAN *(defiantly)*, No! When we made love, it was …

MAN *(contemptuously)*. Oh, Sex. Is that all?

WOMAN. It was more than that.

MAN. Probably. But with the dawn all you felt was hatred.

WOMAN *(Starting to coil again).* That's not fair. You make it sound like a one night stand.

MAN. So it lasted a few days.

WOMAN. It lasted twelve years.

MAN. Twelve years! Not bad. But something went wrong.

WOMAN *(Quietly, making him wait).* Yes.

MAN. Something happened to change it?

WOMAN *(Slowly).* Someone.

MAN. Another woman.

WOMAN. A man actually.

MAN. Deserted for a man.

WOMAN *(she nods).*

MAN. That must have been a bit of a bombshell.

WOMAN. Blew my life apart.

MAN. And not done much for your ego either.

WOMAN. Not a lot. *(She rises and crosses to the side table where the photo has caught her eye again.)*

MAN. Were you married?

WOMAN. We couldn't be. Not then.

MAN. He was married already.

WOMAN. He? ... *(turning to face the room)* Jumping to conclusions. SHE went off with a man.

MAN. Ah!

(The woman wanders around the room again anticlockwise during the next section, picking up objects and examining the furnishings, vaguely turning to the room each time she speaks.)

MAN. Remembering?

WOMAN. Trying to forget.

MAN. Love's roots go deep, don't they?

WOMAN. It hurts like hell.

MAN *(Heartfelt)*. Betrayal has that effect.

WOMAN. You speak like one who knows?

(There is no response from the man.)

WOMAN. You were betrayed?

MAN. Let's talk about you.

WOMAN. Bored with that now.

MAN. I'm not. Tell me about her.

WOMAN. I don't want to talk about it.

MAN. But surely talking helps.

WOMAN *(she has arrived upstage)*. Why do you think I'm moving house?

MAN. You tell me.

WOMAN. You mean you really can't guess.

MAN. Tell me just the same.

WOMAN. I want to forget, damn it!

(He does not respond. After a pause, slowly)

I need to forget. *(She crosses pensively to the settee and slumps down onto it.)* Hampstead is so full of memories. The house reeks of them. Every room screams out at me; claws at me. There is no escape. But memories are like an oil slick contaminating everything it touches . They cling to anything that they come into contact with. I don't want to pollute this place.

MAN. But you can't help carrying memories with you, can you?

WOMAN. Maybe, but at least here I can start afresh, begin healing.

MAN. Perhaps.

WOMAN. Of course I can … if you let me.

MAN. What've I got to do with it?

WOMAN. It seems you come with the place. A sitting tenant.

MAN. And that's a problem for you?

WOMAN. It depends on you.

MAN. As I have said, I can do nothing. It's up to you.

WOMAN. I get the feeling that you have the power to make my life here happy or miserable.

MAN. What makes you think I care one way or the other?

WOMAN. You care.

MAN. And why should I? What makes you so special?

WOMAN. For a stranger and a ghost, *(Rising and moving slightly towards the man who seems to be clearer to her.)* I beg your pardon, a shade, you are remarkably blunt.

MAN. I was trying to be helpful.

WOMAN *(turning away)*. Helpful! You know the meaning of the word.

MAN. Then you haven't been listening.

WOMAN. I heard you being insulting.

MAN. So what did I say?

WOMAN *(Still turned away)*. You suggested that you couldn't care less about me.

MAN. Did I? Think about it.

WOMAN. You asked me what I thought made me so special… *(dawning)* Ah! I see … what does make me so special?

MAN You'd be surprised.

WOMAN *(Turning back)*. So am I special?

MAN. Oh yes.

WOMAN *(She suddenly stares at the man.)* My God, you are much clearer now. You almost look solid.

[THE LIGHTS DIM TO BLACK OUT. AS THEY COME BACK UP THE WOMAN IS SITTING ON THE SETTEE AND THE MAN IS SITTING NEXT TO HER]

MAN.   You have still haven't told me about your love affair. How on earth did you come to fall in love with another woman?

WOMAN. What a stupid question.

MAN.   What's stupid?

WOMAN. You don't choose who you fall in love with. It just happens.

MAN.   And how did it happen for you?

WOMAN. I met her through a friend.

MAN.   An old friend?

WOMAN. No, not really. Just someone I knew. She reckoned I needed cheering up and invited me to a party at the nurses' home.

MAN. What nurses' home?

WOMAN *(getting up and moving to the other chair).* I'd really rather not talk about it.

MAN.   You've gone so far. Why not get it off your chest?

WOMAN. I haven't got anything to get off my chest. That's the silly part of it.

MAN. None the less, tell me about it.

WOMAN. If I must. I was found one night in a pub in Truro at closing time, unconscious. It seems that I had been drinking all day, perhaps for several days. How I'd bought the drink I don't know. When they found me I had no money, no bag and no identification. I could remember nothing. Not even my name. They took me to A & E and then to a clinic to dry out. That's it.

MAN. Go on.

WOMAN. I was given the name Denise, as it seemed vaguely familiar. They decided that the amnesia was brought on by some sort of emotional trauma and probably not helped by alcohol poisoning.

MAN. And you've remembered nothing since.

WOMAN. No.

MAN. How strange.

WOMAN. Strange?

MAN. Yet another past you've forgotten.

WOMAN. That was a part of this life that I can't remember. You said this house was to do with a past life.

MAN. I said nothing of the sort. You were the one that suggested that idea.

WOMAN. And you agreed.

MAN.   What I actually said was "that's one way of putting it." Just a working hypothesis.

WOMAN. So which is the truth?

MAN.   That is still for you to find out.

WOMAN. You are a pain in the arse.

MAN.   And you it seems are an alcoholic.

WOMAN. No. That binge was a one off. I drink socially but I don't need it.

MAN.   So you met this woman at a party.

WOMAN. Penny. Yes. We hit it off from the start. I was looking for somewhere to live and she had a spare room in her flat. I moved in. It was as simple as that.

MAN.   And that's where you've been ever since.

WOMAN. Oh no. When I got promotion we bought a house together.

MAN.   What job were you doing?

WOMAN. Admin at the hospital. It seems I had a talent for it.

MAN.   You did well then.

WOMAN. I got to head of department in under four years.

MAN.   Four years!

WOMAN. Right place, right time.

MAN. And this ... Penny, did you fancy her from the start?

WOMAN *(rising and crossing down right)*. What's it to you?

MAN. I'm just exploring your sexuality. I mean am I safe? You really do prefer women?

WOMAN *(Turning and snapping at him)*. You'd be safe whatever. *(Calmer)* No I can't actually remember meeting a man that I fancied and, yes, I suppose I do prefer women, if you must know.

MAN. I see you're back to confuse men again.

WOMAN *(Suspiciously)*. What do you mean by that?

MAN. It doesn't really matter

WOMAN *(Advancing on him)*. Oh yes it does. Tell me what you mean by, 'confuse men again'.

MAN. You'll remember in due course.

WOMAN. Not that old line again. It's getting to be very boring.

MAN. The rules remain the same. It's all down to you.

(Pause)

WOMAN. You now seem as solid as I am and that's a worry.

MAN. Oh yes I haven't been so solid for a long time. But why should that worry you?

WOMAN *(walking around him)*. Should I decide to take this place, you could be a bit difficult to explain away to friends and neighbours. Will I be stuck with you as a lodger?

MAN. I don't think that will be a problem.

WOMAN Won't they be able to see you?

MAN. Highly unlikely.

WOMAN. Why won't they be able to see you? You seem pretty solid to me.

MAN. They won't see me because I won't be here.

WOMAN. You mean you'll try to keep out of the way.

MAN. No, I'll be long gone.

WOMAN *(brightening)*. You're going to leave?

MAN. In due course.

WOMAN *(Closing on him again and indicating the door)*. Well don't let me keep you.

MAN. But that's just what you're doing.

WOMAN. How's that?

MAN. You're the one controlling events.

WOMAN. So what must I do?

MAN. Remember.

WOMAN. How does that help?

MAN. You need to remember me.

WOMAN. OK, let's see if I've got this right. Once I've solved the mystery of you, you will be gone.

MAN. A consummation devoutly to be wished.

WOMAN *(Moving to stand behind the chair. A slightly far away look in her eye)*. You've said that before.

MAN. Have I? I don't remember.

WOMAN. Not today. It belongs with the house and my memories.

MAN. Really?

WOMAN. Yes, it was your catch phrase.

MAN. My what?

WOMAN. Something you were always saying. Your own pet cliché.

MAN. How boring.

WOMAN *(Moving down stage left, not looking at him)*. I suppose so but I think it was one of the things I loved about you.

MAN. So you remember that too, do you?

WOMAN. Remember what?

MAN. You remember that you loved me.

WOMAN *(disturbed)*. No! ... I mean ... I don't know.

MAN. But you implied that you remembered things that you loved about me.

WOMAN *(more agitated)*. I don't know. I really don't.

MAN. But you must do. *(rising)* You said that you remembered.

WOMAN. Leave me alone. You're confusing me.

MAN *(moving slightly towards her)*. You are confusing yourself. Whether you want to or not, you are remembering.

WOMAN *(Crossing to stage right to get away from him)*. I can't remember what didn't happen. Somehow you're playing tricks with my mind.

MAN. So long as you deny it, you'll remain confused.

WOMAN. It wasn't me. It didn't happen.

MAN. Oh yes it did.

WOMAN. For Christ's sake …

MAN *(Gradually moving towards her, slowly and soothingly)*. Let go.

WOMAN. NO!

MAN *(still moving towards her)*. Let go and remember.

WOMAN. *(Sitting on the down stage arm of the settee)* I don't want to.

MAN. You're so nearly there.

WOMAN *(clasping her hands to her head)*. NO, no, no!

MAN. Remember … Just remember.

WOMAN *(Leaping up and backing up stage away from him).*
Leave me alone, God damn you. LEAVE ME ALONE.

MAN.   That, I can't do. *(He sits on the settee again)*

(She runs to the door. She stops with her hand on the knob. Turns and looks at him for a moment as he sits staring ahead.)

WOMAN *(Then crying hysterically and shouting).* Leave me alone. Please, please, please leave me alone.

(She rushes up the stairs as the lights dim to blackout. As the lights come up again the Man is still sitting on the settee. After a few moments we see the woman slowly coming down the stairs. The Man doesn't look round but seems to know that she is there)

MAN.   Feeling better now?

WOMAN *(From the stairs).* The bedroom is just as you said, exactly as I remember.

MAN. Your brother always kept it that way till he died.

WOMAN. My brother? … Yes Georgie. *(She spots the picture on a table, crosses quickly to it and picks it up.)* His picture. It's still here.

MAN   *(Standing).* And me?

WOMAN. Laurie. Dear Laurie

(She goes to him as if to embrace an old friend but he moves away.)

MAN. It seems that you have a lot more to remember. What was your name?

WOMAN *(Smiling as the memory comes to her).* Bernice.

MAN. No wonder Denise felt familiar, Denise for Bernice.

WOMAN. Yes I suppose so, but most people called me Bunny.

MAN. But not George.

(She is now standing centre stage.)

WOMAN *(thoughtfully).* No … *(brightening at the thought)* No. Georgie called me Rabbit, his Rabbit.

MAN. You and Georgie were very close, weren't you?

WOMAN. Oh yes.

MAN. Brothers and sisters tend to squabble. Did you?

WOMAN. No, never.

MAN. You'd tease him though?

WOMAN. No, I don't think so.

MAN. What about the song that you used to sing?

WOMAN. Song? What song?

MAN. The nursery rhyme about his name?

WOMAN. Oh yes, of course.

(She sings as she moves down stage.)

'Georgie Porgy Pudding and Pie

Kissed the girls and made them cry.

When the boys came out to play

Georgie Porgy ran away.'

But my Georgie never ran away. Georgie always looked after me. It was my earliest memory. He was two years older than me but he always played with me. He used to get quite jealous when other children came to play and God help anyone who hurt me.

MAN.   Time to remember some more. Do you remember The Big House?

WOMAN. Oh yes, old Mrs Farrington used to let us play in the grounds. She lived alone, no children of her own, so she enjoyed having us around. She was like a grandmother to us. Mother was always apologizing to her. Said we took advantage of her good nature but I liked to think that we were important to her. When we were tired of playing games she was always there with lemonade and cakes. The grounds backed onto ours. You can see The Big House through the window at the back

(She crosses to the dining room door, opens it and looks in.)

It's not there. There are houses but where's The Big House?

MAN.   It was sold off when she died about seven years ago and they pulled it down and put up those houses.

WOMAN. What about the lake?

MAN.   Oh yes, it had a lake, didn't it?

WOMAN. We used to swim there in the summer.

MAN. And that was where it first happened wasn't it?

WOMAN. Where what happened?

MAN. Do I have to paint a picture? Hot summer afternoon. Boy aged 15, girl aged 13, they strip off and go for a swim.

WOMAN. Stop it! I remember.

MAN. Well, what happened?

WOMAN *(lapsing into a coy little girl voice)*. No! That's private.

(It is as though she has regressed to childhood again.)

MAN *(moving towards her)*. Today it's for telling.

WOMAN *(petulant little girl)*. Don't want to.

MAN *(gently cajoling)*. Bunny, you have to.

WOMAN *(Crossing stage right)*. I shan't.

MAN. It has to come out.

WOMAN *(turning to face him)*. Why?

MAN. Because you need to remember it all.

WOMAN *(turning down stage)*. But I do remember. So I don't need to talk about it.

MAN *(Moving towards her again)*. Take it from me, you need to talk about it. Or do you want me to tell it?

WOMAN. No! You'll just make it sound dirty. I couldn't bear it sounding dirty.

MAN. And wasn't it?

WOMAN. NO! *(pauses, then looking at the picture that she is still holding)* It was a glorious day, very hot. It was our special corner of the lake. Where we used to go skinny dipping. We had been there for about an hour. Georgie had got out and was sunbathing on the shore. As I got out, Georgie stood up. He was so tanned, almost as brown as his eyes. It struck me how slim and muscular he was. I'd never noticed before. He almost shone where the sunlight picked up his sun bleached hair, especially the hair on his front. Somehow I was no longer looking at my brother. Frightened by the strange way that he was looking at me, I was suddenly aware of my nakedness. I ran off. Of course, he ran after me. Part of me believed that he mustn't catch me and I ran harder, but somehow I wanted to be caught more than anything else in the world. For a moment the exertion of running eased the dread. I told myself it was only the game of chasing each other we had played so many times before. And as he caught me and we tumbled to the ground, for just a few frail moments it was that same innocent romp of teasing, tickling, wriggling laughter that we both knew so well. Then our eyes met and everything changed.

MAN. And you let it happen.

WOMAN. I accepted it with open arms.

MAN. You must have known it was wrong? Unnatural?

WOMAN *(smiling).* For others may be, but for us it was as natural as life itself.

MAN. You were having regular sex with your brother. If nothing else it was illegal.

WOMAN. I had shared my body with him as we shared everything else.

MAN. You ran that risk!

WOMAN. It was vital to us. We knew fate was on our side when I didn't conceive, how ever many times we made love. Georgie said that it was our guarantee that we were right and everyone else was wrong.

MAN. Your parents, didn't they suspect?

WOMAN. We had to be careful, of course. We knew it had to be our secret.

MAN. How did you keep it from them?

WOMAN. It wasn't that hard, at least to begin with. Mother and Father both had their jobs so we were able to be alone almost as often as we liked and the risk of discovery added spice to it. I remember once mother saying to us, "Sometimes, to hear you two talk, it's like listening to an old married couple".

MAN. You said that it wasn't hard to begin with? What changed?

WOMAN. Dad decided to run his business from home so that he was there more often than not. It was the summer, when he first started working from home, so we were always able to go to the lake. It was a wonderful summer but as the days grew cooler, it was harder and harder to find time together.

MAN. So you took bigger risks.

WOMAN. After everyone was in bed we would go to each other, sometimes, my room sometimes his. We were almost caught once when we fell asleep in each other's arms. I'd locked the door, thank God. It was mother trying the handle that awoke us. Georgie hid in the wardrobe as I got up to let mother in. She was surprised to find the door locked but I said that Georgie had been playing practical jokes and I'd locked the door as a precaution. Mother was much too intent on what she wanted to say to think anything more of it.

MAN. I bet that cooled your ardour.

WOMAN *(she glares at him angrily, then decides to ignore it).*
It was hard to accept. But by now we were so close that he could touch me with his eyes with a sensuality as real as any touch of his hand and I believed that I could do the same.

MAN. But that could never be enough really, could it?

WOMAN. You're right. The need grew.

MAN. And love finds a way.

WOMAN. Why am I telling you all this? It's none of your damned business.

MAN. It's the only way that you'll be rid of me.

WOMAN. See yourself as a father confessor, do you?

MAN. Do you need one?

WOMAN. No! I'm ashamed of nothing.

MAN. Why, then, did you feel the need to hide it?

WOMAN. Don't be naïve.

MAN. So you had a problem. How did you solve it?

WOMAN. It was quite easy in the end. Georgie had just got his driving licence, so he always offered to drive me to wherever I needed to go. He said it was to get driving experience and to make life easier for the parents. Of course he always drove us to parties. We only ever stayed a while then made our excuses. It was a big car.

MAN. It was a fast car too, wasn't it.

WOMAN. Yes, but Georgie wasn't a racer.

MAN. But your father was, wasn't he?

WOMAN *(lightly)*. Oh yes. We were always telling him to slow down.

MAN. Driving too fast is dangerous.

WOMAN. That's what we kept saying to him.

MAN. But he didn't listen, did he?

WOMAN. No. ... *(gasps as she remembers)* Oh my God, how could I have forgotten?

MAN. They died in that accident, didn't they?

WOMAN. Yes.

MAN. And suddenly you were on your own together.

WOMAN. We were devastated.

MAN. But I bet you didn't waste a moment though, did you?

WOMAN. That's horrid. Of course we turned to each other for comfort. We'd lost our parents. Wasn't it natural?

MAN. I can see you now. Curled up together, crying your eyes out.

WOMAN. I cried but Georgie was so strong. He said someone had to be.

MAN. I bet he did. But you inherited the house and a tidy sum, didn't you?

WOMAN. That wasn't important.

MAN. Face it. It couldn't have worked out better: young, comfortably off, your own private love nest, with no one to hide your secret life from.

WOMAN. We'd lost our parents. You don't get over things like that easily.

MAN. But you managed to in the end.

WOMAN. Of course the pain wore off and eventually it was idyllic. But there was still the guilt.

MAN. You felt guilty?

WOMAN. Guilty that losing them had made my life with Georgie so perfect. It didn't seem right. At times I almost believed that I had somehow brought about the accident by wishing that Georgie and I could be alone.

MAN. Now isn't that strange.

WOMAN. Why strange?

MAN. All in good time. Well, you had eight years of uninterrupted bliss, before another problem turned up, didn't you?

WOMAN. Laurie, don't do this.

MAN. Don't do what? Remind you that I came into your life. That I fell desperately in love with you.

WOMAN. And I with you.

MAN. But not enough it seems.

(She tries to sit beside him to embrace him. He rises and moves away.)

No keep away. Don't touch me.

WOMAN. Oh yes I wanted you so badly.

MAN. At the time, I believed that. I could never understand why you wouldn't commit yourself. Always excuses, reasons why not, reasons for waiting. And fool that I was, I couldn't see the truth, the real reason why not. George!

WOMAN. You were forcing me to decide between you.

MAN *(With bitter sarcasm).* Between incest and a healthy relationship. Some decision.

WOMAN. I know it seems like that, but for me it was like cutting off an arm or a leg.

MAN. And that wouldn't have been a good thing?

WOMAN. No!

MAN.   So stringing me along was easier.

WOMAN. No, Laurie, you don't understand.

MAN.   Oh, I understand. You were like Siamese twins that would die if separated. You were never going to agree to marry me.

WOMAN. Given time I could have brought Georgie round.

MAN.   Who are you kidding? George hated me. That was plain as day. But I thought that he saw himself as a substitute father determined that his daughter should not marry the wrong man. It never crossed my mind that the two of you were lovers.

WOMAN. I was sure that I could win Georgie over.

MAN   *(laughing)* What did you envisage, a ménage à trois?

WOMAN. I really believed that he'd love me enough to let me go.

MAN.   Oh Bunny … Yes, you really were that naïve. That at least is true.

WOMAN. But I did love you.

MAN.   I'm sure that you thought you did, but you loved him more.

WOMAN. Oh, Laurie, *(She tries to embrace him again and he slips away)*

MAN.   No, keep away.

WOMAN. But it's not true. I really did love you.

MAN.   Bunny, on the Saturday you swore to me your undying love and on the Sunday morning I walked in on the two of you fucking. Can you imagine what that felt like?

WOMAN *(a long silence, far away remembering).* Oh yes. I remember that look in your eyes.

MAN   *(quietly).* And George ... he didn't even break rhythm. He just shouted in between humps Well nobody ... bloody well ... invited you ... to watch, ... Laurie. He actually climaxed as he said my name and all you did was giggle.

WOMAN. Well,, I was embarrassed.

MAN.   Embarrassed! That's it? You felt embarrassed?

WOMAN. What do you want me to say?

MAN.   I felt humiliated and I was just an observer. *(She says nothing)* But even then I didn't stop loving you.

WOMAN. You did. You said you were going to expose us.

MAN.   I would never have done that. I just wanted to shock you into breaking with George and to come away with me. I was so in love with you, I thought I would have forgiven you anything.

WOMAN. But Georgie believed that you would betray us. He said that it would mean up to seven years in prison for both of us. Apart. Probably never being able to be together again.

MAN.   And you believed him over me.

WOMAN. Oh yes, I believed him. I was terrified. I'd seen the expression of horror on your face and I knew it was the end for us.

MAN. Horror at what I'd seen. Disgust that your brother had betrayed you. Loathing of him. Loathing of the act, certainly. But not of you. I loved you. I could never have hurt you.

WOMAN. Georgie convinced me that the only future we had was each other. He said that, now you knew about us, it was all we had left.

MAN. And I had to die.

WOMAN. George said it would be painless.

MAN. But you did it. You, who professed to love me took the responsibility of killing me.

WOMAN. Georgie said he would kill himself rather than go to prison. And if I didn't silence you, that is exactly what would happen. Georgie told me what to do. He said that you had to die and that if I loved you it was down to me to do it. I was the only one who could get close enough.

MAN. That was his insurance. Once you had killed me, he had a hold over you. There would be no risk of you leaving him for someone else after that.

WOMAN. I almost hoped that you would leave straight away.

MAN. Yes, if I had left the house you couldn't have done it. Then why on earth do you think I stayed if I didn't still love you?

WOMAN. Georgie said it was to give us a false sense of security..

MAN. Oh, he had you eating out of his hand, didn't he? I didn't go because I still hoped to win you over and I knew it would take time.

WOMAN. How was I to know that?

MAN. I loved you. I could see you were trapped and, fool that I was, I wanted to get you away from a sick relationship.

WOMAN. Laurie, it wasn't sick. Oh maybe in the eyes of the world, people who didn't know what we meant to each other, maybe legally too, but for us it was natural, for us it was right.

MAN. If it was so right, how come you actually considered leaving him for me … if you ever did?

WOMAN. You were different.

MAN. I wasn't your brother, you mean.

WOMAN. In a sense that's true but not the way you mean. You were different. It was like nothing I'd ever felt before. Georgie was my brother and we were very close. We had let that closeness have a physical expression. But it was still only brother and sister. It was just the children in us.

MAN. And of course you didn't enjoy it.

WOMAN. Of course I enjoyed it but still I was doing it for Georgie, it was what he wanted, what he needed. It was mine to give, so how could I deny him this special gift? I owed him.

MAN. You didn't owe him anything.

WOMAN. I owed him everything. He had always looked after me. He never let me down.

MAN. Listen to yourself Bunny. There was no way, that you could ever have left George.

WOMAN. Laurie you were different. As I said, Georgie and I were not much more than over excited, affectionate children. With you, for the first time I could see a grown up life, a future with a family where sex meant the real thing. It was going to be life changing and I wanted it.

MAN. Well, that's what you said you wanted the night that you climbed into bed with me and we made love. How do you imagine I could make love as we did, if I hated and loathed you?

WOMAN. I imagined that it was part of the act. You felt that you had to keep living the part if you were to trap us. And I knew if our plan was to work, I had to encourage you. It had to be good.

MAN. And you were good. You were very good. And when we stopped you said that you were sure that your Georgie would come round but, until then, we had to keep our relations secret, which was why you couldn't stay long. You said you had to get back to your own bed in case Georgie discovered us. It never crossed my mind that George knew you were with me; that he had put you up to it. That must have rankled knowing what we were up to. As you knelt by the bed, whispering all the words that you knew that I wanted to hear, you were setting the poison in place, under the bed. Carbon tetrachloride. Two more illicit meetings. Two more chalices of poison and in five days I died in my sleep, poisoned by inhaling the fumes that would leave no trace. You talked of betrayal earlier. Well I learnt betrayal from a mistress of the highest order.

WOMAN. Laurie I did love you. That's why it had to be me that killed you.

MAN. That's a great consolation.

WOMAN. Georgie said that it was a special act of devotion.

MAN. He certainly knew what buttons to press, didn't he? But then he'd had a lifetime to learn them.

WOMAN *(desperate to embrace him)*. Oh Laurie darling you must understand.

MAN. *(pushes her violently on to the settee)*. I have told to you keep your hands off me.

WOMAN. Oh Laurie, LAURIE.

MAN *(Standing over her)*. I remember the funeral. I was there too you know, watching you both. The little trip out onto the lake in the old boat. George's version of a burial at sea. All very theatrical. Rolling me over the side, weighted down, and then George swimming to the bottom as my body sank to ensure that it was well entangled in the waterweed before cutting away the ropes from first the body and then the stones that he'd used to weigh me down. Nobody would suspect the stones without the ropes. When I was missed and if the lake was dragged, it would seem like a swimming accident. A simple drowning.

WOMAN. What can I say?

MAN. The irony is, that that was the night you finally ran away from home. Do you remember that?

WOMAN. Yes.

MAN. Do you remember why?

WOMAN. The funeral and the thought of what I'd done.

MAN. Are you sure that was all?

WOMAN. What else?

MAN. How about the other murders.

WOMAN *(sitting up)*. What do you mean? What other murders?

MAN. At least after dumping my body you shed some tears.

WOMAN. Yes.

MAN. Inconsolable. Not that George tried to console you. For once George was unsympathetic.

WOMAN. He was very angry with me. We had a row, the first ever. He said that it was my fault that you had to die. I should never have invited you to stay with us.

MAN. And it all came out didn't it?

WOMAN. What? I can't remember anything else.

MAN. You will! What did he say next

WOMAN *(unconvincingly)*. I don't know.

MAN. Oh yes, you do. He said he would kill anyone who came between the two of you, didn't he?

WOMAN. Yes.

MAN. And what little bombshell did he add.

WOMAN. No! No! Please don't make me!

MAN. You have to say it.

WOMAN. He said he would kill them like he always had.

MAN. And you asked him what he meant by that, didn't you?

WOMAN. Yes.

MAN. And he told you exactly what he meant, didn't he?

(Bernice is suddenly reliving that night. Holding the picture to herself she follows an invisible George around the room.)

WOMAN. Oh Georgie how could you. Not Mum and Dad.

MAN. He had access to the family car. He knew what a reckless driver your father was. He sabotaged the brakes. It was just too much, wasn't it?

WOMAN. Not Mum and Dad, Georgie, say you didn't. Not Mum and Dad.

MAN. You couldn't live with it.

WOMAN. What do you mean, you did it for us. Never for us. Not a thing like that.

MAN. You decided to leave.

WOMAN. What are we going to do?

MAN. He rejected you that night.

WOMAN. Why must I go to my room? … No, please don't leave me alone tonight.

MAN. It was the first time that he got you wrong. He should have kept you by his side.

WOMAN. But I need you tonight more than I ever have.

MAN. You were able to get out of the house without him seeing you leave.

WOMAN. I forgive you, Georgie. Please forgive me. I want you so much.

MAN. You drank a lot and left with your bags full of more booze than clothes.

WOMAN. I need you to hold me. Please Georgie! Please!

MAN. By the time they found you in that Truro pub, you had closed the door on the past.

WOMAN *(Awakening from the past).* What's happening?

[AS THE SCENE ENDS THE AREA LIGHTING GRADUALLY FADES TO TOTAL BLACKNESS BUT FOR A SPOTLIGHT THAT FOLLOWS LAURIE]

MAN. It's all over, Bunny. You've made it and it's all over … bar the shouting that is.

WOMAN. What have you done to me, Laurie?

MAN. I've done nothing but set the wheels in motion.

WOMAN. Wheels? Wheels, what wheels?

MAN. The wheels of justice.

WOMAN. But something is happening to me.

MAN. Yes, justice is putting things to rights.

WOMAN. But I feel strange, like I'm fading away.

MAN. That's only to be expected.

WOMAN. But I don't like it.

MAN. It's been happening ever since you walked in here.

WOMAN. I don't understand.

MAN. You have been returning to your rightful place, with George, where you belong.

WOMAN. But Georgie died. You said so.

MAN. Haven't you learnt anything from tonight?

WOMAN. You mean that I am becoming like you are?

MAN. Like I was. You are now a very light shade and I am solid.

WOMAN. But I want to leave.

MAN. I am the one who is leaving and it was you who made it possible.

WOMAN. You tricked me.

MAN. No. You came to this house because you needed to. You were drawn to it. You hoped to find peace here. To begin with, you didn't know why because your conscious mind had blanked out. But deep down you hoped Georgie would take you back. But you didn't know that your Georgie was dead too. Ever since you left that night he longed for you, but he was haunted by me. He never saw me but the deed haunted him. I kept myself in his mind night and day. One morning, he took the boat out and dived down to see if my remains were still there. I had become so vivid in his mind he was beginning to doubt that I was dead. He never found the body but became entangled in the weeds himself and drowned. He joined me to haunt this house.

WOMAN. Georgie, darling Georgie, is he really here.

MAN. Where else would he be? In fact none of this would have been possible if darling Georgie had been against it. Another betrayal. Well I must be off.

WOMAN. You're not going to leave me here. I'm frightened.

MAN. I have no choice.

WOMAN. But I'm frightened. I'm so frightened.

MAN. You brought it all on yourself.

WOMAN. Please take me with you.

MAN. It was always out of my hands but now it is out of yours as well. We have come too far.

WOMAN. I can hardly see you. I'm scared. Please help me, Laurie.

MAN. Go to Georgie. I'm sure that he is waiting for you.

WOMAN. Where am I? Oh God, where am I?

(Mr Ignis enters and stands silhouetted in the door.)

MR IGNIS. All finished here?

MAN. Yes, Mr Ignis, quite finished. Good-bye, Bunnie. *(He crosses to the door. Looking back)* It was good to see you again.

MR IGNIS. Would you like me to lock up?

MAN. Yes please, Mr Ignis, and thank you, thank you so much. *(EXITS followed by Ignis who closes door behind him)*

(The set is in total darkness)

WOMAN *(her voice, childlike again, is distant but clear)*. Georgie, are you here? Georgie, where are you? Please come to me. I'm lost, Georgie. I'm so lost.

(singing their song, her voice fading all the time)

'Georgie Porgy Pudding and Pie

Kissed the girls and made them cry.

When the boys came out to play

Georgie Porgy ran away'

(and there is a slow curtain)

PRODUCTION NOTES

The significance of the estate agent Mr Ignis should not be over looked. Ignis is of course Latin for fire.

Where a minimal set is desirable two elements are vital.

The main door has to be realistic, solid and able to be slammed convincingly. Secondly the foot and the first few steps of the stairs need to be visible. THE GIRL's going up to escape what is happening and her resigned descent is important. Other doors etc need only be suggested. The other requirements are the settee and easychair, a piece of furniture for the picture of George and other items to stand on plus anything to suggest the rooms furnished state that THE GIRL explores.

Suggested set for Shades

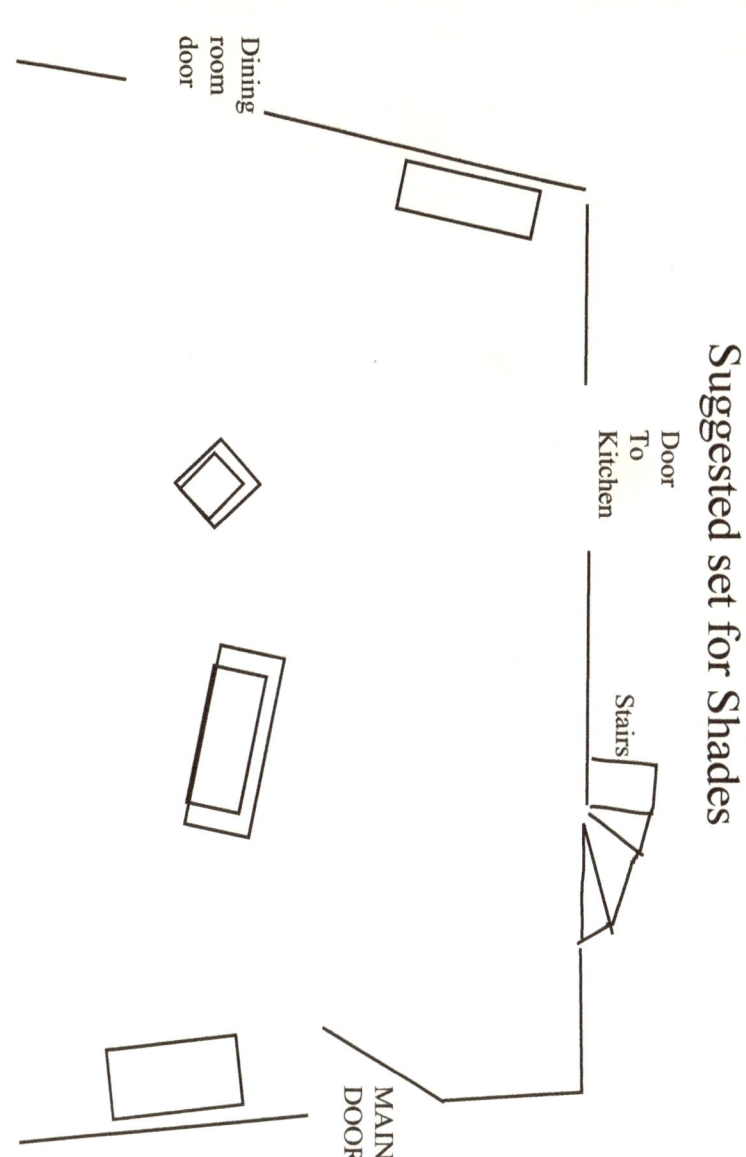

Where a minimal set is desirable two elements are vital.

The main door has to be realistic, solid and able to be slammed convincingly. Secondly the foot and the first few steps of the stairs need to be visible. THE GIRL's going up to escape what is happening and her resigned descent is important. Other doors etc need only be suggested. The other requirements are the settee and easychair, a piece of furniture for the picture of George and other items to stand on plus anything to suggest the rooms furnished state that THE GIRL explores

Properties and furnishings

1 settee.
1 easy chair.

Other general furnishing to include a table displaying pictures etc.

A framed picture of Georgie.

Other family pictures.

Fire Circle Publishing

Publishers of Fiction, Non Fiction, Biography, Poetry, Plays and Anthologies.

The Authors we publish are selected from an elite group.

FIRE CIRCLE PUBLISHING was set up in 2013 by the chairman of **PHOENIX WRITERS' CIRCLE** as facility to help members of the group and sister group **MOLE VALLEY SCRIPTWRITING GROUP** to get their work established in print.

So quality control can be managed, currently, only the work of members of Phoenix Writers' Circle and affiliated groups will be considered for publication. On the other hand membership will not guarantee publication.

CONTACT DETAILS
Website:-

http://www.firecirclepublishing.uk/

Fire Circle Publishing, 9a Craddocks Parade, Ashtead, Surrey KT21 1QL

TEL 01372 817353

E-mail:- tim@firecirclepublishing.uk

Barton's Bookshop

One of Britain's best independent traditional booksellers.
A shop not to be missed if you are in Leatherhead.

2 Bridge Street, Leatherhead, Surrey. KT22 8BZ
Website:- http://www.bartonsbookshop.co.uk/
E-mail:- sales@bartonsbookshop.co.uk
Tel:- 01372 362 988

All FIRE CIRCLE Published books are available through Barton's Bookshop either in the shop or on line.

ALSO BY KENNETH CLELLAND AND PUBLISHED BY FIRE CIRCLE

Also from Fire Circle Publishing

STEPPING INTO VERSE
BY
HUGH TIMOTHY

Contained within **Stepping into Verse** is some of my earliest verse, some items dating back 40 years or more. This is one reason why I chose the title. Those early poems represent my first steps into verse. My wish that the book might introduce others to the fun and joy of verse was my second reason for the title.

Often, when I read poetry, I feel I would like to know the story behind the verse; how it came to be written. I believe that knowing this can increase one's understanding of the verse. So to make this collection a bit different I decided to do just that.

The poems are not set in any chronological order, and whilst their arrangement is not altogether random, the connection between one item and another is occasionally somewhat tenuous and abstract.

SHAPES

By

HUGH TIMOTHY

SHAPES is Hugh Timothy's second collection. It is made up from three short unpublished pamphlets, and years of other work. Many of the individual poems have appeared in poetry magazines and other publications and include some prize winning poems.

His first collection *Stepping Into Verse* was self published and sold out and is being reprinted by Fire Circle Publishing re-edited and with added poems, to coincide with the launch of *Shapes* and **the Mole Valley Arts Alive Festival October 2014.**

His poetry covers a wide range of subjects and poetic genre.

*"Life throws shapes at us that we have to negotiate, hard edged shapes, flexible shapes and complementary shapes"*HT